Corporate Knowledge for Government Decisionmakers

Insights on Screening, Vetting, and Monitoring Processes

RYAN ANDREW BROWN, DOUGLAS YEUNG, DIANA GEHLHAUS, KATHRYN O'CONNOR

Prepared for the Office of the Secretary of Defense
Approved for public release; distribution unlimited

 NATIONAL DEFENSE RESEARCH INSTITUTE

For more information on this publication, visit www.rand.org/t/RRA275-1

Library of Congress Cataloging-in-Publication Data is available for this publication.

ISBN: 978-1-9774-0545-6

Published by the RAND Corporation, Santa Monica, Calif.

© Copyright 2020 RAND Corporation

RAND® is a registered trademark.

Preface

Corporations and the federal government face a common challenge: vetting to decide who can be trusted with valuable and sensitive information. The research described in this report was designed to study vetting and monitoring challenges across the corporate lifecycle, mapping the different vetting and monitoring processes used by a corporate sample to determine areas where the U.S. government might consider implementing some similar practices from the business world—whether strategic or tactical—to improve the efficiency and effectiveness of U.S. government vetting and monitoring.

This research was sponsored by the Security, Suitability, and Credentialing Performance Accountability Council Program Management Office and conducted within the Cyber and Intelligence Policy Center of the RAND National Security Research Division (NSRD), which operates the National Defense Research Institute (NDRI), a federally funded research and development center sponsored by the Office of the Secretary of Defense, the Joint Staff, the Unified Combatant Commands, the Navy, the Marine Corps, the defense agencies, and the defense intelligence enterprise.

For more information on the RAND Cyber and Intelligence Policy Center, see www.rand.org/nsrd/intel or contact the director (contact information is provided on the webpage).

Contents

Figures

Tables

Summary

Introduction

The U.S. government's (USG's) screening and vetting process seeks to ensure that those who work for or on behalf of the federal government can be trusted to serve in positions where they may handle classified or otherwise sensitive information, material, people, or property that could pose risks to national security or public trust if not properly protected. As of 2020, the Trusted Workforce 2.0 efforts are transforming the federal vetting process to improve performance and efficiency. Certain corporate sectors share common attributes with the government that are highly relevant to their need for rigorous vetting of prospective employees. To improve vetting and monitoring in the federal government, we looked to examples from private industry. The study had two key objectives: (1) identify key strategic and tactical approaches used by corporations in the technology, pharmaceutical, finance, and gaming sectors to screen, vet, and monitor employees to limit damage from internal and external threats; and (2) highlight elements of these approaches that could potentially be applied to USG vetting and monitoring. To accomplish these objectives, we conducted background research consisting of a literature review, relevant research from current and ongoing RAND Corporation projects, and consultations with colleagues. We also conducted field data collection consisting of interviews and site visits with both large and small corporations in the above corporate sectors, analyzing the results to identify practices that could increase the efficiency and effectiveness of the federal personnel security vetting process.

Findings

Background Research

We found that one significant difference between the USG personnel security vetting process and practices in the corporate realm is that corporations generally control the talent management process from its very early stages through termination of employment. In contrast, individual agencies, contractors, and other USG entities (including, for example, military branches and units) manage the hiring process, with the majority of agencies handing over personnel security vetting to a central authority in the USG. While corporations sometimes "outsource" various parts of the talent lifecycle to outside contractors, they generally maintain relatively more control and oversight of the overall human resources (HR) life cycle.

Because corporations are independent (with the exception of needing to comply with federal and state laws), they may selectively experiment with technological approaches in different parts of the talent lifecycle, picking and choosing those that are more appropriate for the volume and diversity of roles they have available, their specific risks and vulnerabilities, their stage of and goals for corporate growth, and so forth. Corporations are thus more agile and flexible in the way they conduct (and change) processes for screening, vetting, and monitoring. In contrast, the centralized federal process seeks to find a common set of investigative and monitoring practices to cover a very wide variety of roles and access to information.

Still, as noted, private corporations and the USG share many of the same challenges and even some of the same adversaries (for example, China is a geopolitical competitor that has attempted to steal corporate intellectual property). Thus, when reviewing lessons learned from our corporate interviews for the second objective, we focused on broad trends and approaches that could be adapted by the federal government as it pursues personnel security vetting reform, rather than on specific technologies or technical approaches.

Field Research

Using a mix of phone, video, and in-person data collection (site visits), we interviewed security and HR personnel from a total of nine corporations across the technology, pharmaceutical, finance, and gaming corporate sectors. We began by building a sampling strategy stratified by corporation characteristics according to whether the corporation was legacy or *nonlegacy*, which we defined using several rough attributes: *Legacy* corporations were defined as large, established corporations or those that had traditionally done business with the USG, while *nonlegacy* corporations were smaller, potentially startups, as well as those that did not perform much work for the USG. Table S.1 describes the corporate sample we recruited and the method of data collection for each corporation.

We found that interviewees most consistently mentioned specific employee roles as presenting the greatest risk: (1) high-level executives whose behaviors could expose the corporation to reputational risk or vulnerability via blackmail; and (2) HR, information technology, or

Table S.1
Corporations by Sector, Type, and Method of Data Collection

Corporation Type	Technology	Pharmaceutical	Finance	Gaming
Legacy	Tech hardware producer (<500 employees) • in-person interview	Large biotech corporation (~15,000 employees) • phone interview	Two large banks (~20,000 employees) • one by site visit and one by phone interview	Two legacy casinos (25,000–100,000 employees) • phone interviews
Nonlegacy	Small (<50 employees) startup online content producer • video interview	Pharmaceutical startup (<1,000 employees) • site visit	Small financial tech start-up (<500 employees) • phone interview	*Skipped in favor of legacy casinos because of difficulty in recruiting nonlegacy casinos*

other administrative personnel with access to client and personnel data, as well as (in some cases) corporate intellectual property. The most frequently mentioned motivation for nefarious employee behavior was disgruntlement and vengeance, which could lead to theft of corporate property or even threats to workplace safety.

Corporations in our sample exhibited considerable diversity in screening, vetting, and monitoring practices, much of which was industry-specific and some of which was more related to legacy versus nonlegacy status (corporate size and stage of growth). For example, smaller and newer corporations preferred less structured, more flexible and informal screening and vetting processes, with any malfeasance handled on a case-by-case basis. Larger organizations in established, highly regulated industries, such as finance and pharmaceuticals, tended to have more structured processes, given the constant need to follow federal and state regulations.

Few corporations in our sample used newer artificial intelligence (AI) and machine learning (ML) automated analysis approaches for prehire screening, vetting, or employee monitoring—approaches that have received considerable media attention recently. Employing such approaches seems to require the integration of corporate functions and overall corporate agility. Corporations that did employ AI or ML techniques cautioned that any automated analytics needed constant monitoring and contextualized interpretation with a "human in the loop."

Insights

Based on our background research and interviews, we derived the following insights to help inform the USG for personnel screening, vetting, and monitoring. **Proper sorting of cases is challenging but necessary to preserve a balance between maintaining operational capacity and eliminating critical threats.** Our respondents described the increasing trend toward carefully sorting potential threats into cases that can be addressed with HR or other approaches versus cases that require immediate punitive action. Potentially derogatory information on those who work for or on behalf of the federal government calls for a wide range of response options.

Intelligence should be shared inside and outside the organization. HR and security professionals described a variety of creative ways to fuse and share intelligence to rapidly identify and address emerging threats. Such fusion is subject to legal and regulatory constraints, especially when conducted by the USG. Emerging technologies may help lower the labor costs of intelligence fusion. However, these are still in their infancy and should be employed with caution and human monitoring.

Keeping a human in the loop is essential. For the foreseeable future, automated algorithms to detect risky or nefarious behavior by applicants or those who work for or on behalf of the federal government need significant, consistent oversight by HR or security professionals. Much as algorithms struggle to properly understand nuance in social media posts, using ML to sort human behavior into categories (such as flagging nefarious behavior) is rife with risks for error and bias.

Taking a "whole of community" approach to identifying and mitigating threats helps share the labor burden and improves effectiveness. Corporations reporting successful threat detection and mitigation use a customized, flexible, hands-on approach. While fully decentralizing the USG clearance process is impossible, the USG could develop requirements for critical information and task corporate intelligence, HR, and security functions to provide that information with the appropriate caveats and context.

Looking to the future, the potential threats posed by those who work for or on behalf of the federal government are growing in their diversity and potential severity, prompted in part by the growing sophistication of foreign adversaries seeking to place or recruit such threats inside the United States. In the face of these challenges, traditional approaches to screening, vetting, and monitoring based largely on human labor will no longer be sufficient. However, the wide variety of AI- and ML-powered "solutions" currently offered in industry (or suggested by academic studies) need to be systematically tested or assessed in a real-world context to determine how they operate and how effective they are in successfully identifying threats.

Failure to adopt emerging approaches to screening, vetting, and monitoring could leave the USG exposed in the evolving threat environment. But failing to undertake a systematic review and assessment of these approaches could lead to wasted investment or to the acquisition of ineffective systems that miss important threats, misidentify harmless behaviors as threats, or potentially deepen existing bias and discrimination in current HR systems.

Acknowledgments

We thank the sponsor of this research, the Security, Suitability, and Credentialing Performance Accountability Council Program Management Office, for thoughtful guidance throughout this project, including but not limited to assistance engaging corporate interviewees. We also thank Sina Beaghley and Rich Girven for their invaluable feedback and guidance, and our reviewers David Luckey and Larry Hanauer for their insight and feedback to improve the report. Finally, we thank our interviewees, without whom this research would not have been possible.

Abbreviations

AI	artificial intelligence
ATS	application tracking system
CE	continuous evaluation
CRM	customer relationship management
CV	continuous vetting
DCII	Defense Central Index of Investigations
DCSA	Defense Counterintelligence and Security Agency
DSS	Defense Security Service
FBI	Federal Bureau of Investigation
FDA	U.S. Food and Drug Administration
FDIC	Federal Deposit Insurance Corporation
GAO	U.S. Government Accountability Office
HHS	U.S. Department of Health and Human Services
HIPAA	Health Insurance Portability and Accountability Act
HR	human resources
IP	intellectual property

ISP	Investigation Service Provider
ML	machine learning
NBIB	National Background Investigation Bureau
NDAA	National Defense Authorization Act
OPM	Office of Personnel Management
PAC	Performance Accountability Council
PII	personally identifiable information
PMO	Program Management Office
SII	Security/Suitability Investigations Index
USG	U.S. government
VERIS	Vocabulary for Event Recording and Incident Sharing

CHAPTER ONE

Introduction

The U.S. government's (USG's) screening and vetting process seeks to ensure that those who work for or on behalf of the federal government can be trusted to serve in positions where they may handle classified or otherwise sensitive information and material. Currently, this process is both time- and resource-intensive and may not be optimally designed to catch insider threats.[1] Backlogs in cases waiting to be investigated for personnel security vettings were creating long delays in granting and renewing security clearances, resulting in regular delays of a year or more.[2] Though that processing timeline and the backlog overall has been reduced significantly as of 2020,[3] such delays can have detrimental impact on national security and public trust by slowing the pipeline of qualified individuals who have been approved to serve in sensitive positions of trust and by hindering the monitoring of trusted insiders. And yet, despite the time and resources devoted to vetting, the system has, in a number of cases, failed to identify individuals who presented risk in several high-profile incidents. These include information leaks

---

[1] For supporting research focused on continuous evaluation (CE), see David Luckey, David Stebbins, Rebeca Orrie, Erin Rebhan, Sunny D. Bhatt, and Sina Beaghley, *Assessing Continuous Evaluation Approaches for Insider Threats: How Can the Security Posture of the U.S. Departments and Agencies Be Improved?* Santa Monica, Calif.: RAND Corporation, RR-2684-OSD, 2019.

[2] Luckey et al., 2019; Nicole Ogrysko, "'Time to Change the Rules' for the Security Clearance Process, Its Leaders Say," *Federal News Network*, August 7, 2018.

[3] See Aaron Boyd, "Security Clearance Backlog Hits Long-Awaited 'Steady State,'" *Nextgov*, January 22, 2020.

(e.g., Edward Snowden, Chelsea Manning),[4] as well as violent attacks (e.g., Nidal Hassan, Aaron Alexis).[5]

The USG is not alone in facing the challenge of screening and vetting individuals to guard against insider threats. Certain corporate sectors share common attributes with the government that are highly relevant to their need for rigorous vetting of prospective employees. For instance, tech and pharmaceutical corporations handle specific forms of sensitive information—e.g., personally identifiable information (PII), Health Insurance Portability and Accountability Act (HIPAA)-compliant, financial, proprietary, or even classified information—and must protect valuable intellectual property (IP), such as software code or patented drug formulas.

On average, corporations face an annual cost of $8.76 million because of losses from insider threats,[6] and the frequency of insider threat incidents has increased over time.[7] Recent threats to corporations from insiders range from the leak of Google's work with China via Project Dragonfly[8] to the leak of 100 million customer accounts from Capital One by a single employee.[9]

The rising severity of insider threats—including the ways that employees can be used to access corporate data and assets by competing corporations or even international adversaries—has led to increased corporate attention directed at ways of screening and vetting employees, as well as at monitoring and responding to threats in real time. For example, Verizon has developed the VERIS (Vocabulary for Event

4   Jan Wolfe, Joseph Ax, David Ingram, Kevin Drawbaugh, and Jonathan Oatis, "Factbox: Long History of U.S. Leakers to Media Facing Charges," Reuters, August 4, 2017.

5   Matt Vasilogambros and National Journal, "The Navy Yard Shooting Could Have Been Prevented, Review Finds," The Atlantic, March 18, 2014. For additional information on the "Violent Insider," see Luckey et al., 2019.

6   Ponemon Institute, 2018 Cost of Insider Threats: Global, Boston, Mass.: ObserveIT, April 2018, p. 2.

7   Ponemon Institute, 2018, p. 3.

8   Jennifer Elias, "Report: Google Management Scrambles to Contain Employee 'Uproar' over China Project," Silicon Valley Business Journal, August 3, 2018.

9   Jane Grafton, "Famous Insider Threat Cases," GURUCUL blog, September 5, 2019.

Recording and Incident Sharing) framework and structured data set,[10] as well as a recent report detailing the types of employees, motivations, and incidents that are common across corporate insider threats.[11]

Thus, both public and private entities face the challenge of how to handle a high operational pace of vetting and monitoring, because of the expansion of sensitive data and the proliferation of threats worldwide. And, like the USG, corporations also must balance the public relations benefits of transparency with the need for operational security regarding how employees and external threats are assessed and monitored. The Security, Suitability, and Credentialing Performance Accountability Council (PAC) Program Management Office (PMO) and the broader federal government thus confront a similar vetting challenge to corporations: needing to decide who can be trusted with valuable and sensitive information, as well as how to detect emerging threats that those who work for or on behalf of the federal government can pose.

Objectives and Approach

Given recent calls to improve vetting and monitoring in the federal government, looking to examples from private industry is a logical step. However, it is important to ensure the validity of comparisons between federal and private industry vetting and monitoring needs, constraints, and possibilities. In other words, this comparison requires a systematic research approach; practices from private industry cannot be adopted uncritically and expected to work in the federal context. This project, therefore, sought to take an initial step by mapping vetting and monitoring processes used by a corporate sample to determine areas where the USG might consider implementing some similar practices from the business world—whether strategic or tactical—to improve the efficiency and effectiveness of USG vetting and monitoring. The two

---

[10] Verizon, "VERIS: The Vocabulary for Event Recording and Incident Sharing," webpage, 2019.

[11] *Insider Threat Report: Out of Sight Should Never Be out of Mind*, New York: Verizon, 2019.

key objectives were (1) to identify key strategic and tactical approaches used by corporations in the pharmaceutical, technology, finance, and gaming (gambling) sectors to screen, vet, and monitor employees to limit damage from internal and external threats; and (2) to highlight elements of these approaches that could be potentially applied to USG vetting and monitoring.

Delivering useful insights to the USG requires some degree of comparability in the threats that corporations try to avoid by vetting and monitoring individuals, as well as comparability (or at least potential comparability) in processes used by the government and the corporate sectors. To do this, we conducted interviews and site visits with both large and small corporations in several corporate sectors, analyzing the results to identify practices that could increase the efficiency and effectiveness of federal employee vetting and monitoring. Crucial for this task was ensuring that we spoke to appropriate corporations, which, for example, would be (1) under significant ongoing threat from adversaries or competitors, (2) taking active steps to screen, vet, and monitor employees to limit the risks posed by employee behavior, and (3) generally regarded as leaders in security practices by others in their industry. We also wanted to ensure that we covered diverse vetting and monitoring practices.

Working from the resulting understanding of federal demands and existing processes for vetting and monitoring, the RAND team sought to augment this framework with similar practices from relevant corporate sectors. To do this, we conducted interviews and site visits with both large and small corporations in several corporate sectors, analyzing the results to identify practices that could increase the efficiency and effectiveness of federal employee vetting and monitoring. Crucial for this task was ensuring that we spoke to appropriate corporations, which, for example, would be (1) under significant ongoing threat from adversaries or competitors, (2) taking active steps to screen, vet, and monitor employees to limit the risks posed by employee behavior, and (3) generally regarded as leaders in security practices by others in their industry. We also wanted to ensure that we covered diverse vetting and monitoring practices.

Taken together, the purpose of these research tasks was to collect interesting processes or insights that might be applicable to the USG. For several reasons, these insights are broad by design. First, they are intended to apply to the overall national security and public trust enterprise, rather than to serve as specific recommendations for the Defense Counterintelligence and Security Agency (DCSA). Second, because of recent changes, the USG personnel security vetting process is a moving target for comparisons with corporate practices. Third, rather than evaluate the effectiveness of corporate practices, this research sought mainly to surface ideas that the government could consider adopting. For example, we asked questions about perceived risk around specific employee roles, or how emerging technologies such as artificial intelligence (AI) and machine learning (ML) are used for employee screening and vetting. We did not attempt to verify the effectiveness of these practices, which would have required additional and potentially sensitive information about corporate outcomes (e.g., security violations). As in national security and positions of public trust, corporations must seek to protect not only their sensitive information but also their own security and intelligence "tradecraft." As expected, some corporations declined to participate, perhaps reluctant to divulge the details of their own internal practices. However, drawing on related previous work, we were able to identify a sufficient number of private industry partners who were willing to share their practices to assist the USG, and from whom we drew insight. Therefore, we could not evaluate or verify the impact of screening and vetting steps that corporations did or did not undertake. Rather than describing our findings regarding corporate practices as recommendations that the federal government undertake, this report presents them as insight into measures that could be considered for adoption.

Organization of This Report

This report describes corporate vetting practices that may offer insights for how the USG could improve employee vetting. As context for these corporate vetting insights, Chapter Two provides background information about USG vetting processes, including general steps and time frames and a broad overview of how hiring, screening, vetting, and ongoing monitoring are conducted in the corporate world. Chapter Three describes the methods used to select relevant corporations and the resulting corporate sample. Chapter Four presents the findings from our corporate interviews. Chapter Five concludes with observations of general and emerging trends from our field research and insights on promising practices to address gaps and inefficiencies.

CHAPTER TWO

Overview of U.S. Government and Corporate Screening and Vetting Procedures

This chapter begins by providing a framework for understanding how the USG screens potential hires to detect, avoid, and mitigate potential threats to the USG and the national interest. We first provide a broad overview of the USG vetting process, focused on the provision and monitoring of security clearances specifically. This broad overview is based on publicly available materials and consultations with USG officials. It describes the personnel security vetting process as it stood in 2018. Notably, starting in 2019, the USG screening and vetting process was, and is still, undergoing a significant transformation, including both a transfer of authority and development of new capabilities. In a separate section, we provide information on this transition and the form it is starting to take.

We then provide a broad overview of how hiring, screening, vetting, and ongoing monitoring is conducted in the corporate world—with an emphasis on how emerging technology is used in the corporate domain. This overview is based on research and interviews RAND has conducted through other projects, as well as a recent review of how new technology is being used in the *human resources (HR) lifecycle*—that is, in the process of attracting employees who are a good fit to corporate roles and who present relatively low risk to the corporation—and in training, monitoring, evaluating, and terminating these employees as needed.

We conclude the chapter with some conclusions for drawing inferences from the corporate world for the federal government. We do this by reviewing similarities and differences in the USG personnel

7

security vetting process versus screening, vetting, and monitoring in the corporate world.

Personnel Security Vetting as Conducted by the Office of Personnel Management

In this section, we describe the personnel security vetting process[1] as it was conducted by the Office of Personnel Management (OPM), an independent agency within the USG. On June 24, 2019, President Donald Trump signed an executive order transferring investigative authority to a new agency, the DCSA.[2] We describe impending changes linked to this transfer of authority and associated new processes (called *Trusted Workforce 2.0*) in the following section of this chapter.[3]

The U.S. Department of Defense outlines the procedures used for personnel security vetting in the *Department of Defense Suitability and Fitness Guide*.[4] The suitability and fitness process involves four steps: preinvestigation, investigation, adjudication, and postadjudication (see Figure 2.1). The investigation process is conducted by an authorized Investigation Service Provider (ISP); 95 percent of executive branch agencies use the shared service provided by DCSA. Other components of the investigation process—including searches of OPM's Security/Suitability Investigations Index (SII) and the Defense Central Index of Investigations (DCII); review of Federal Bureau of Investigation (FBI) investigation, criminal history, and fingerprint files; and any other agency checks deemed necessary for a position or in relation to the

---

1   The USG vets employees for positions of public trust and national security. Vetting for public trust is called *suitability screening* and shares many elements of vetting for national security.

2   Nicole Ogrysko, "Trump Makes Security Clearance Transfer Official with Executive Order," *Federal News Network*, April 24, 2019a.

3   Nicole Ogrysko, "The Future of Continuous Evaluation Is Just About Here, and It Has a Different Name," *Federal News Network*, September 6, 2019b.

4   U.S. Department of Defense, *Department of Defense Suitability and Fitness Guide: Procedures and Guidance for Civilian Employment Suitability and Fitness Determinations Within the Department of Defense*, Washington, D.C., updated July 28, 2016.

Figure 2.1
Mapping of Personnel Security Vetting Process

Preinvestigation	Investigation	Adjudication	Postadjudication
• ~80 days • Hiring process • e-QIP initiation	• ~126–340 days • Review e-QIP • Interim determination • Investigation	• ~29–33 days • Favorability decision made	• Employee notification • Appeals process

NOTE: e-QIP = Electronic Questionnaires for Investigations Processing.

individual's background—are performed by the USG. All investigations contain National Agency Checks, which include the SII, DCII, FBI fingerprint, and FBI investigation files, citizenship and legal status, and other agency checks deemed necessary for a position or in relation to the individual's background. Other components of the investigation process may include a credit check; personal subject interview; employment, education, and residence reviews; reference interview; and public record searches covering five to ten years. The requirements are based on the risk and sensitivity level of the position.

In the process of personnel security vetting, the USG looks for and considers a variety of personal characteristics, situations, and relationships that might lead to behaviors that would put national security or public trust at risk, including employee misconduct, criminal or dishonest conduct, alcohol abuse, narcotic use, sexual misconduct, and financial irresponsibility. Total time required to grant secret and top secret clearances reached a maximum of more than 300 and 500 days (respectively) but as of the fourth quarter of 2019 were reported to take 181 days for secret clearances and 295 days for top secret clearances.[5] The investigation step, which involves contracted work assigned to ISPs, takes the longest and averages about 80 percent of the total time required.

---

5   Lindy Kyzer, "How Long Does It Take to Process a Security Clearance? (Q4 2019)," *ClearanceJobs*, November 20, 2019a.

Recent Personnel Security Vetting Process Reform

Several changes in the personnel security vetting process are currently underway. These changes were prompted in part by long wait times for security clearances,[6] as well as by well-known failures of USG security programs to predict or prevent leaks of sensitive information and violent attacks by insider threats.[7] A recent large data breach that OPM experienced also played a role in these changes,[8] as did the perception that the personnel security vetting process has become outdated and fails to take advantage of modern technological advances and HR practices.[9]

These issues prompted the U.S. Government Accountability Office (GAO) to release a series of reports highlighting risks and performance issues with the personnel security vetting process, including OPM's vulnerability to cyber threat,[10] delays in the processing of security clearances,[11] the need for specific plans to implement continuous evaluation,[12] and the continuing status of personnel security vetting

6   Kyzer, 2019a.

7   Mariano Castillo, "Other Leakers: What Happened to Them?" CNN, January 2, 2014; Tom McMurrie, "Insider Threats: Taking a Holistic Approach to Protecting Agency Data," Federal News Network, December 27, 2017.

8   OPM, "Cybersecurity Resource Center: Cybersecurity Incidents," webpage, 2015.

9   Joseph Marks, "Antiquated Security Clearance Process Earns a Spot on the GAO's High-Risk List," Nextgov, January 25, 2018; Luckey et al., 2019.

10   GAO, "Information Security: Agencies Need to Improve Controls over Selected High-Impact Systems," GAO-16-501, Washington, D.C., June 21, 2016; GAO, "Information Security: OPM Has Improved Controls, but Further Efforts Are Needed," GAO-17-614, Washington, D.C., August 3, 2017a.

11   GAO, "Personnel Security Clearances: Additional Actions Needed to Ensure Quality, Address Timeliness, and Reduce Investigation Backlog," GAO-18-29, Washington, D.C., December 12, 2017c; GAO, "Personnel Security Clearances: Additional Actions Needed to Implement Key Reforms and Improve Timely Processing of Investigations," GAO-18-431T, Washington, D.C., March 7, 2018.

12   GAO, "Personnel Security Clearances: Plans Needed to Fully Implement and Oversee Continuous Evaluation of Clearance Holders," GAO-18-117, Washington, D.C., November 21, 2017b.

as a high-risk issue for the USG for both efficiency and data security reasons.[13]

On April 24, 2019, President Trump signed an executive order establishing the DCSA, which took over all responsibilities from the Defense Security Service (DSS) (responsible for Department of Defense security clearances before 2005); the order transferred the responsibility for federal background investigations from OPM and the National Background Investigations Bureau (NBIB) to the DCSA—and ordered the transition to happen no later than September 30, 2019,[14] including the transfer of NBIB personnel and resources to the DCSA.[15]

The USG is also simultaneously implementing the Trusted Workforce 2.0 initiative, which is designed to organize, simplify, and modernize personnel security vetting and to introduce continuous vetting (CV) to replace the burdensome and time-consuming periodic reinvestigation of individuals with security clearances.[16] Additionally, the 2020 National Defense Authorization Act (NDAA) further mandated elements of security clearance reform suggested by the GAO and others, including (1) requiring a plan to reduce security clearance backlogs to 200,000 cases; (2) setting a milestone of 30 days or less for a secret clearance and 90 days or less for a top secret clearance by December 2021; (3) creating a transparent, accessible online portal documenting progress in the clearance process for individual cases by December 31, 2023; and (4) requiring an update on the status of Trusted Workforce 2.0, including an update on how technology will be used

13 The security clearance process was listed as high risk from 2005 to 2011 and was moved back onto this list in 2018. See pp. 158–162 in GAO, 2018.

14 Donald J. Trump, Executive Order on Transferring Responsibility for Background Investigations to the Department of Defense, April 24, 2019.

15 DCSA Office of Public Affairs, "Background Investigation Mission Moving to DoD," press release, Office of Personnel Management, July 2019.

16 Ten percent of individuals with clearances are still expected to need full periodic reinvestigation ("Push to Change Security Clearance Policies Underway," *FEDweek*, August 21, 2019).

for insider threat monitoring.[17] So, reform is well underway for the USG personnel security vetting process.

The Corporate Talent Lifecycle

In this section, we provide a broad overview of how the corporate world conducts hiring to maximize employee performance and to both assess and reduce the risk that employees present to corporations. This overview is based on previous background research and interviews conducted at RAND, as well as additional background research for this project. Given the increasingly prominent place of data-enabled technologies, this overview also focuses on the use of technology in corporate hiring, screening and vetting, and monitoring.

The corporate talent lifecycle offers lessons and potential insights into how technology is being integrated in pre- and posthiring practices. The nature and role of technology used in private-sector talent management is growing and evolving, and trends suggest new technologies are being adopted at each stage of the recruiting, hiring, and monitoring process. Figure 2.2 illustrates the corporate talent lifecycle, as well as how technology is being integrated in the various stages.

The corporate talent lifecycle model consists of 12 stages. These stages map the major phases of interactions with potential hires and employees—identification, engagement, and attraction (Find, Attract, Engage, and Apply in Figure 2.2); screening, interviewing, and hiring (Screen, Interview, Assess, and Hire in Figure 2.2); and employee management (Onboard, Train, Monitor, and Transition in Figure 2.2). The employee lifecycle is also referred to as "from cradle to grave" or "from hire to retire."

Although the corporate world has used technologies in employee management for some time, the last decade has seen a more prolific integration of emerging technologies into all stages of the

17 Lindy Kyzer, "Security Clearance Reform in the NDAA," *ClearanceJobs*, December 16, 2019b; Nicole Ogrysko, "Congress Catches Up on Security Clearance Modernization Efforts in NDAA," *Federal News Network*, December 12, 2019c.

Figure 2.2
Corporate Talent Lifecycle and Use of Technology

Tech in Corporate HR

- Data mining
- ML profiling of ideal candidates

- Online account
- Screening "games"
- Social media and other data
- ML-automated screening

- New hire dashboard and metrics
- Training "games"
- Corporate online social communities

| Find | Attract | Engage | Apply | Screen | Interview | Assess | Hire | Onboard | Train | Monitor | Transition |

- Social media
- Online talent communities

- Chatbots
- Experiential websites

- Video interviews and facial expression analysis
- Interview "games"
- Smartphone interview scheduling and notifications

- Ongoing monitoring of business data (email, chat, text messages, etc.)
- ML profiling for risk of malfeasance, espionage, etc.

SOURCE: Summary of gray and white literature from human resources and recruiting, including Mike Kofi Okyere, "Recruitment Analytics: How Data Helps Achieve Better Results," webpage, Recruiter, July 30, 2018; Josh Bersin, "Why People Management Is Replacing Talent Management," LinkedIn, December 29, 2014; and Michael Stephan, David Brown, and Robin Erickson, "Talent Acquisition: Enter the Cognitive Recruiter," Deloitte Insights, 2017.

employee trajectory and talent management.[18] In each of the stages, these technologies are reshaping how HR functions are executed. They are also reshaping the candidate experience—engagement and communication with the corporation—and, as a result, forcing corporations to prioritize having a positive corporate brand, identity, and reputation.[19]

Technology in recruiting for some firms begins right in the identification, engagement, and attraction stages. Firms—and many third-party vendors—have developed algorithms to mine public, internal, and purchased data to find potential applicants, usually with specialized skills and experience. Many of these algorithms attempt to match individuals with an *ideal candidate*, attributes determined by a combination of current employee skill sets and more-general skills or experience demanded by the firm.[20] They may also leverage hiring platforms such as LinkedIn and Monster to access resumes and other potential applicant pools.

More frequently, corporations are also reaching out to applicants instead of waiting for applicants to find them.[21] Most corporations have pages across social media platforms and maintain a presence on specialized sites (e.g., Github) to engage and initiate conversations with prospects. Corporations increasingly view attracting talent as tied to corporate brand and reputation and, as a result, are coordinating internally with marketing.[22] As part of improving the customer (applicant) experience, corporations are moving toward experiential and interactive websites for the careers page. Some corporations also create online closed communities within their website to build resume reposi-

18   Anthony Grijalva, "7 HR Technologies for Managing the Employee Lifecycle," *Employee Benefit News*, 2020.

19   Stephan, Brown, and Erickson, 2017.

20   Peter Cappelli, "Your Approach to Hiring Is All Wrong," *Harvard Business Review*, May–June 2019.

21   Cappelli, 2019.

22   Sarah Bengochea, "Putting Brand and Challenge at the Heart of Talent Acquisition," *Blog & News*, Avature, 2020.

tories and keep technical expertise engaged even if there are no current openings.[23]

Once a prospect decides to apply, technology continues to keep applicants engaged. For instance, application chatbots can answer questions about the position or application process.[24] Many corporations have automated communication and scheduling features available through their application tracking system (ATS) or customer relationship management (CRM) system to keep the process moving. Communication can happen by email, phone, or, increasingly, nontraditional media such as text message.[25]

In the screening, interviewing, and hiring stages, the use of video and games have proliferated. Many corporations use video interviewing to screen applicants. More corporations are also using the video feed to conduct psychometric or sentiment analysis on the applicants, looking for certain personality traits or attributes. Incorporating games into the hiring process is also becoming more common, known as *gamification* in hiring,[26] to evaluate an applicant's logic or reasoning skills, or to assess whether their thought process fits with what the employer is looking for.

Finally, in the employee management domain, corporations are harnessing the data footprint left by employees. Some firms have capabilities to actively monitor email, internet browsing, and social media, among other techniques. According to a December 2018 report from Glassdoor, some employers are also using sensors to track employee movement and location, and office webcams to monitor workplace activity.[27]

23 *2019 Talent Trends Report*, Atlanta, Ga.:: Randstad Sourceright, 2019.

24 John Dawson, "6 Best Recruiting Tools of 2019," *AI for Recruiting: News, Tips, and Trends* blog, Ideal, January 10, 2019.

25 Jena McGregor, "Your Next Job Interview May Start with a Text," *Washington Post*, November 20, 2018.

26 Chiradeep BasuMallick, "Gamification in Recruitment: All You Need to Know," *HR Technologist*, November 30, 2018.

27 Andrew Chamberlain, "Job Market Trends: Five Hiring Disruptions to Watch in 2019," webpage, Glassdoor, December 2018.

Corporations Are Selectively Applying Technologies Within the Lifecycle

Importantly, implementation of these technologies, even proven ones, is not consistent across the private sector. For example, most organizations use a software platform such as an ATS or CRM to manage applications during the hiring process, as well as to manage other HR functions. However, corporations vary widely in the level of sophistication of their platforms. Platforms on the market range from having basic functionality for storing and tracking applications to being fully integrated with other HR, finance, and customer-facing applications.[28]

The variation in adoption is still greater for emerging technologies.[29] Larger corporations that receive thousands of applications annually and corporations that have niche or specific hiring needs may be more likely to make the investment. These corporations may also select which technologies fit their hiring and retention needs, choosing technologies to assist in some stages of the lifecycle but not others. They may also apply the technologies to only certain categories of workers, if they are large and hire across many levels of skills and experience—for example, conducting psychometric analysis for public-facing employees or creating and maintaining an online community for interested talent with specific technical skills.

Of all the technologies mentioned, several have raised public concerns about the possibility for discrimination or bias. These including ML and other data mining to identify and initially screen candidates, as well as psychometric analysis.[30] As a result, these technologies are more limited in current use. Once these technologies become more proven in their ability to detect threats while minimizing bias, however, they may become more widely implemented.

---

28   G2, "Best Applicant Tracking Systems," webpage, 2020.

29   Erica Volini, Jeff Schwartz, and Indranil Roy, "Accessing Talent: It's More Than Acquisition," *Deloitte Insights*, 2018.

30   Drew Harwell, "A Face-Scanning Algorithm Increasingly Decides Whether You Deserve the Job," *Washington Post*, November 6, 2019.

Conclusions and Lessons for Comparison

One significant difference between the USG personnel security vetting process and practices in the corporate realm is that corporations generally control the talent management process from its very early stages through termination of employment. In contrast, individual agencies, contractors, and other entities in the USG (including military branches and units, for example) manage the hiring process, with the majority of agencies handing over personnel security vetting to a central authority in the USG.[31] In turn, the USG uses a variety of other government and contracted entities to complete the personnel security vetting process. While corporations may outsource various parts of the talent lifecycle to outside contractors, they generally maintain relatively more control and oversight of the overall process.[32]

Because corporations operate in a relatively independent manner (with the exception of needing to comply with federal and state laws), they may selectively experiment with technological approaches in different parts of the talent lifecycle, picking and choosing those that are more appropriate for the volume and diversity of roles they have available, their specific risks and vulnerabilities, their stage of and goals for corporate growth, and so forth. Corporations are thus more agile and flexible in the way they conduct (and change) processes for screening, vetting, and monitoring. In contrast, the centralized federal process seeks to find a common set of investigative and monitoring practices to cover a very wide variety of roles and access to information.

As outlined in Chapter One, private corporations and the USG nonetheless share many of the same challenges and even some of the same adversaries (for example, China is a geopolitical competitor that has attempted to steal corporate IP). Thus, when reviewing lessons learned from our corporate interviews, we focus on broad trends and

---

[31] Federal civilian job postings and applications for a wide variety of agencies are also processed through a centralized entity, USAJOBS.

[32] Trusted Workforce 2.0 is moving the USG away from the older model toward a more integrated, corporate model and introducing new processes, such as CE. For example, see Jory Heckman, "ODNI Previews Updated Counterintelligence Strategy, Trusted Workforce 2.0 Rollout," *Federal News Network*, February 5, 2020.

approaches that could be adapted by the federal government as it pursues personnel security vetting reform, rather than on specific technologies or technical approaches.

CHAPTER THREE

Corporate Sample and Methods

This chapter describes how we recruited and interviewed our corporate sample, and how we produced and analyzed data from these interviews.

Multisectoral and Diverse Corporate Sample

For our corporate interviews and site visits, we sought to build a diverse sample that would allow us to identify a wide range of corporate practices. We began by building a sampling strategy stratified by corporation characteristics, using two primary criteria. The first was whether the corporation was *legacy* or *nonlegacy*, which we defined using several rough attributes: *Legacy* corporations were defined as large, established corporations or those that had traditionally done business with the USG, while *nonlegacy* corporations were smaller, potentially start-ups, as well as those that did not perform much work for the U.S. government.

The second criterion was the corporate sector in which the corporation operated. Initially, we intended to focus on the pharmaceutical and technology sectors. We chose these sectors because they had several factors that made them relevant to USG vetting, such as handling various forms of sensitive information (e.g., financial or proprietary data, PII). Later, based on discussions with our PAC PMO sponsor, we added the financial and gaming (i.e., casino) sectors.

Table 3.1 outlines these criteria and the resulting sampling strategy. Combining the four sector types with two legacy types yielded eight possible corporate types. We then began to identify candidate

Table 3.1
Corporations, by Sector and Type

	Tech	Pharmaceuticals	Finance	Gaming
Legacy	In-person interview: legacy tech hardware producer (<500 employees)	Phone interview: large biotechnology corporation (~15,000 employees)	• Site visit: large bank (~20,000 employees) • Phone interview: large bank (~20,000 employees)	Phone interviews: two legacy casinos (25,000–100,000 employees)
Nonlegacy	Video interview: small (<50 employees) startup online content producer	Site visit: pharmaceutical startup (<1,000 employees)	Phone interview: small financial tech startup (<500 employees)	*Skipped in favor of legacy casinos[a]*

a This was because of difficulty in recruiting nonlegacy casinos.

corporations in each of these eight options. In total, we identified and reached out to more than 25 candidate corporations via a variety of means, including LinkedIn, email, conference calls, website forms, and PAC PMO contacts. There was a roughly 60-percent refusal rate (the highest rate of refusals was in the tech sector). Personnel from corporations who refused often cited legal or public relations concerns, while others appeared not to perceive any benefit in participating. In the end, personnel from nine corporations agreed to participate.

Using a mix of phone, video, and in-person data collection, we interviewed security and HR personnel from a total of nine corporations. In two cases, we were able to conduct in-person site visits, including a tour of facilities used for HR and security functions. With the exception of one corporation, we interviewed one person from each corporation. In total, five interviewees performed HR or people operations roles, and six interviewees had security roles. There was one "dual-hatted" respondent who performed both roles. One corporate interview included two individuals with security roles.

Interview Questions Focused on Risk Assessment and Mitigation

Our interview questions were designed to identify corporate practices in two main areas of employee vetting. First, questions about *risk assessment* asked participants about high-risk employee roles and the greatest areas of concern—that is, areas with the greatest potential risk that employee vetting was intended to guard against. Second, questions about *risk mitigation* asked participants to describe approaches to mitigate the risks they had previously identified, including screening or monitoring practices, and any other tools or techniques in use. Table 3.2 provides greater detail on specific interview topics within each of these two areas.

Analysis of Interview Themes

We analyzed data from site visits and interviews by entering it into the Dedoose team-based qualitative coding software for structured thematic analysis. We then coded emergent themes using structured hierarchical coding (see the appendix for the full list of hierarchical data codes). We also summarized overall findings along with trends by

Table 3.2
Interview Topics

Risk Assessment	Risk Mitigation
• What risks can or do employees present to your institution? Please describe the types of risks presented and indicate which are most prevalent, as well as which are most potentially damaging. • Which types of employee roles present the greatest risk? Why?	• What does your corporation do to detect, guard against, and mitigate these risks? • Who executes these functions? • What new technologies, approaches, or strategies have you adopted due to changes in the landscape of data and analytics in the past decade? • How has your screening process changed in the last few years due to data leaks, new and emerging threats, proliferation in data collection and access, or concerns for data privacy?

SOURCE: RAND interview materials.

industry sector, size, and stage (legacy and public versus start-up and private). This data analysis was driven by information on USG vetting and monitoring processes, as described in Chapter Two, to ensure that we were making valid comparisons.

Limitations

Our approach is limited in several ways, as are the inferences that can be drawn from it. Because of constraints imposed by the Paperwork Reduction Act, we restricted our desired sample size to nine corporations. Furthermore, the sampling scope included only corporations that we were aware would meet the sampling criteria, and many corporations declined to participate. Most of these refusals came from corporations in the nontraditional tech sector. For each corporation that did agree to participate, we talked to one or two people who did not represent the same role in each organization. This means that their perspectives likely differed according to their role.

As a result of these limitations, our sample provides a limited ability to depict the overall employee vetting process for each corporation. A fuller understanding would require much more detailed information, corroborated across multiple sources. Furthermore, two to three corporations per sector, of course, cannot fully represent each corporate sector. Thus, the scope of inferences we could make was limited to identifying potential innovations in use within an individual corporation, and from those drawing broader lessons learned from the corporate sector. Additionally, comprehensive comparison between corporate and government vetting is challenging, given that USG screening and vetting is in transition.

In terms of the scope of interview questions, we did not ask about perceived effectiveness of various risk assessment and mitigation practices. Furthermore, we did not ask participants to describe the landscape of external adversaries (foreign actors, competing corporations, etc.) that seek to recruit their employees to their causes. These are both scope limitations of the study.

CHAPTER FOUR

Findings from Corporate Interviews

Types of High-Risk Employees

All interviews and site visits began with a discussion of the type of employee that presented the greatest risk to corporations. Interviewees responded to this question with a combination of employee categories and narratives regarding past incidents. Of course, each industry (and each corporation) structures employee roles differently, owing to different regulatory environments, different corporate operational needs, and different corporate cultures. Thus, rather than present an exhaustive list of the types of risky employees mentioned by each corporation or industry, we identified common themes across interviews regarding how and why employees present risks to corporations. This analysis revealed that employee types and specific stories about employee risk focused on (1) the degree to which employees had access to valuable corporate assets, and (2) the degree to which specific employee roles presented opportunities for loss or compromise of these assets (see Table 4.1).

For example, respondents from the technology, pharmaceutical, and gaming sectors emphasized how the public behavior (or private behavior, if leaked via email hacks or other means) of well-known, high-profile executive leaders could put corporate reputation at risk. Meanwhile, respondents from the technology and pharmaceutical industries—both of which engage in extensive research and development—emphasized how researchers, engineers, and even production staff had access to intellectual property that could greatly harm corporate competitiveness if shared externally.

Table 4.1
Employee Risk Emphasized Most by Respondents from Each Corporate Sector

Type of Risk/Vulnerability	Type of Employee	Technology	Pharmaceutical	Finance	Gaming
Corporate reputation	• High-profile executives	X	X		X
Intellectual property	• Researchers • Engineers • Line production	X	X		
Federal compliance	• Operations • Finance			X	X
Personnel and client data	• HR • Administrative • Information technology	X	X	X	
Cash flow	• Casino floor • Bank tellers			X	X
Products and packaging	• Supply chain • Warehouse			X	X

SOURCE: RAND analysis of corporate interviews.

NOTE: An "X" in each box simply means that interviewees emphasized this risk during the interview. Absence of an "X" in each box does *not* mean there is no risk to corporations in this sector.

The technology, pharmaceutical, and finance sectors all cited the risk presented by HR, information technology, and administrative personnel with access to corporate sensitive data, such as employee records and client accounts. Meanwhile, the financial and gaming sectors—both of which must contend with significant federal oversight—emphasized the degree to which roles involving processing large sums of money presented risks for noncompliance. Both of these industries also noted how *line staff* (i.e., casino floor workers and bank tellers) with significant access to cash presented risk for theft. For the pharmaceutical sector, line staff presenting a similar risk came in the form of those with access to the supply chain (including production staff and warehouse employees) of both packaging and substances with high black-market demand.

Risky Behaviors and Motivations

After discussing the types of employees presenting the greatest risk to corporations, we turned the conversations next to the behaviors that such employees could engage in to cause harm. To make our findings comparable across industries (each of which faces somewhat different threats), we analyzed descriptions of behaviors and narratives of past harm for commonalities in risky behaviors and their underlying motivations. Such behaviors fell along a spectrum from carelessness and accidents to truly nefarious intentions and actions (see Figure 4.1).[1]

The pharmaceutical and finance industries both emphasized that the most common risk came from simple carelessness or negligence—for example, leaving a laptop in an airport—leading to loss of intellectual property or corporate sensitive data.[2] In a similar vein, the technology, pharmaceutical, and gaming industries all described how poor impulse control and/or engagement in immoral or

---

[1] For an alternate categorization of types of insider threats (and their various motivations), see pp. 20–21 in Luckey et al., 2019.

[2] The RAND research conducted by Luckey et al. (2019) also emphasized the importance of negligence in creating national security threats.

Figure 4.1
Spectrum of Motivations and Associated Risks

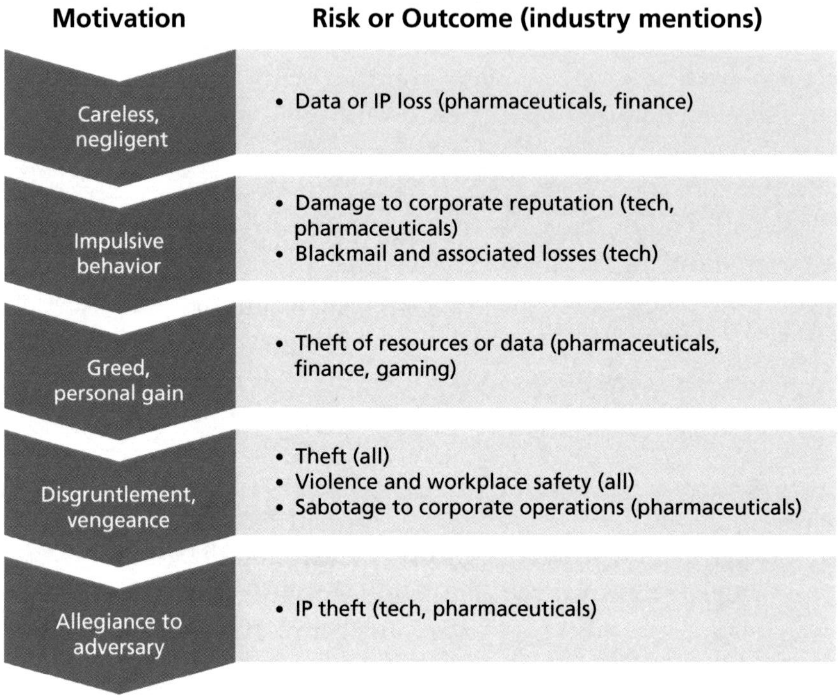

Motivation	Risk or Outcome (industry mentions)
Careless, negligent	• Data or IP loss (pharmaceuticals, finance)
Impulsive behavior	• Damage to corporate reputation (tech, pharmaceuticals) • Blackmail and associated losses (tech)
Greed, personal gain	• Theft of resources or data (pharmaceuticals, finance, gaming)
Disgruntlement, vengeance	• Theft (all) • Violence and workplace safety (all) • Sabotage to corporate operations (pharmaceuticals)
Allegiance to adversary	• IP theft (tech, pharmaceuticals)

SOURCES: RAND analysis of corporate interviews, combined with existing corporate and government models to classify and grade risk and employee motivation. For corporate framework, see *Insider Threat Report: Out of Sight Should Never Be out of Mind*, 2019. For government framework, see PA Consulting Group, *Holistic Management of Employee Risk (HoMER)*, London: Centre for the Protection of National Infrastructure, 2012.
NOTES: Blue arrows indicate the range of motivations discussed, in order of increasing nefarious intent. Bullets show results of these behaviors discussed in interviews, along with the industries that mentioned each. Industries mentioned emphasized each risk. Absence of an industry in any particular bubble does not indicate absence of risk in that sector.

embarrassing behaviors by top executives could harm corporate profile and public relations. These three industries also described how such behavior could be leveraged by adversaries to extort information or resources via vulnerability to blackmail.

Respondents from the pharmaceutical, finance, and gaming industries all described how simple greed or motivations for personal gain led employees to engage in theft of money or resources—or, in some cases, large-scale theft of intellectual property or client data to help competing organizations profit or to secure a role at a competing organization. Respondents in all corporate sectors described how this sort of theft—or, in some cases, deliberate sabotage—were often motivated by disgruntlement toward other individuals inside the corporation and the desire for vengeance of some kind.[3] Similarly, respondents in all corporate sectors spoke of being increasingly aware of the risk for targeted or mass violence from disgruntled or mentally unstable employees. Finally, respondents in the technology and pharmaceutical industries, both of which hold significant intellectual property, described how some cases of intellectual property loss were motivated by allegiance or sympathy to foreign actors.

Prehire Screening and Vetting

This section describes the variety of processes followed by corporations to hire personnel who could be a good match to employment roles and present the lowest risk for improper behavior, commonly referred to as *screening and vetting*. Screening and vetting processes varied widely across the corporations we interviewed, and these differences appeared to be related to the size of the organization and corporate sector.

For all corporations in our sample, screening started with a basic background check of some kind (see Figure 4.2). All checks, at a minimum, included a civil and federal criminal check and Social Security verification.[4] Corporations interviewed across size and sector also

---

[3]   For additional details on employee disgruntlement and its link to insider threat, see pp. 24–25 in Luckey et al., 2019.

[4]   These background checks occurred at different points in the hiring process, with some occurring postinterview and others occurring after a tentative offer was made. This differed by industry, role, and associated statutory requirements. For more information, see Society for Human Resource Management, "Conducting Background Investigations and Reference Checks," webpage, 2020.

Figure 4.2
Corporate Prehire Screening and Vetting

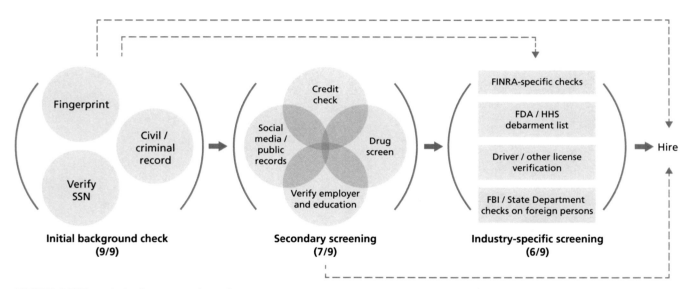

SOURCE: RAND analysis of corporate interviews.
NOTES: Dashed lines indicate that some corporations skipped certain steps. Separate circles in "Initial background check" indicate that these steps were always performed as a set. Overlapping circles in "Secondary screening" indicate that corporations employed one or more of these steps. Separate boxes in "Industry-specific screening" indicate that corporations tended to take one (but not more than one) of these steps. FDA = U.S. Food and Drug Administration; HHS = U.S. Department of Health and Human Services; SSN = Social Security number.

emphasized the importance of screening criminal data for past arrests indicating predisposition to commit workplace violence; seven out of the nine corporations we interviewed mentioned this as a relatively recent and expanding area of concern and focus for their corporations.

From this point, corporate practices diverged (see Figure 4.2). Seven of the nine corporations completed all or some combination of the following: education and employment verification, drug testing, fingerprint checks, credit checks and liens, and a watches and sanctions lists check.[5] Only two (both newer and smaller corporations) described taking none of these steps. For these additional checks, there were different perspectives on which elements were meaningful or predictive of performance, and therefore worth including. For example, one interviewee felt that credit checks were not indicative of job performance, especially since many people struggled with credit during the Great Recession. Interviewees whose corporations did not include them noted the trade-off between time and resources and the uncertain predictive capacity of this additional information.

On the one hand, smaller and newer corporations—especially those in the tech sector—prided themselves on having a minimally time- and resource-intensive process. These interviewees generally stopped with the initial background check. Instead, they were more likely to focus on whether the employee was a good fit for the corporate culture. These corporations included cultural fit as part of the interview and hiring process, although it was generally a subjective or qualitative assessment.

On the other hand, larger corporations in the gaming, pharmaceuticals, and finance industries (six out of our nine corporations interviewed) prioritized meeting multiple legal and regulatory requirements (see Figure 4.2). Some of the interviewees in these sectors represented large corporations that also had to run thousands of checks annually. The representatives we spoke with at these corporations were much

---

5   Watch and sanction lists check for persons who have been put on a global watch list or have a public record in another country for various reasons. For more information, see LexisNexis, "Perform Sanction, PEP and Watchlist Verification with Lexis Diligence," webpage, 2020.

more focused on meeting federal and state requirements for screening and vetting applicants.[6] For example, the financial entities we interviewed were required to comply with Federal Deposit Insurance Corporation (FDIC) Section 19—if they are FDIC-insured—and Regulation Z from the Dodd-Frank Act.[7] Interviewees subject to regulatory oversight on employee screening procedures emphasized that they spent significant time and resources tracking down information from incomplete background checks and on having to consult with the potential hire on any offenses discovered. These interviewees also stated it was difficult to refuse hiring on the basis of noncriminal offenses, because of exposure to legal challenges from potential hires, including claims of discrimination. On top of this, legal differences among states affected such decisions.

Some divergence in screening practices was also specific to select occupations within sectors. For example, the pharmaceutical sector used FDA debarment and HHS exclusion lists to screen out potential hires for production and logistics, motor vehicle checks for drivers, license verification for financial traders, and additional screening for senior executives. One technology corporation interviewed sent all foreign resumes to the U.S. State Department for verification that they were not foreign spies that could have access to valuable research, while one pharmaceutical corporation consulted with the FBI on applicants with potential allegiance to specific U.S. foreign adversaries. Many of these additional screenings were driven by legal requirements.

---

6   Otherwise, they risk penalties and other fines. For example, Citigroup was fined $1.25 million in July 2019 for complying with federal banking regulations but not federal securities regulations in screening employees. See Michelle Ong and Mike Rote, "FINRA Fines Citigroup Global Markets Inc. $1.25 Million for Failing to Appropriately Fingerprint or Screen Employees over Seven-Year Period," press release, Financial Industry Regulatory Authority (FINRA), July 29, 2019.

7   Any financial entity involved in the trading or selling of securities must also be compliant with FINRA employee screening rules as backed by the U.S. Securities and Exchange Commission. Public Law 111-203, Dodd-Frank Wall Street Reform and Consumer Protection Act, July 21, 2010.

Interestingly, another emerging screening practice, psychometric profiling and sentiment analysis at the prehire stage,[8] was not prevalent in our sample.[9] One corporation interviewed did use psychometric analysis as part of initial screening to more quickly filter through applications selected for interviews. This corporation noted the importance of personality in making a successful customer service employee. Other corporations were aware of psychometric and sentiment analysis but did not employ this capability at the time of interview.

Interviewees also differed on standards for screening contractors. Some contractors were subject to the same screening processes as employees, while others were not screened at all. Some of this variation had to do with risk mitigation, and some had to do with legal requirements. For example, contractors dealing directly with pharmaceuticals or personally identifiable data create risk for the corporation that makes intensive screening of contractors important as a risk mitigation strategy. Depending on the role of the contractor, screening contractors was sometimes legally required. For example, contractors in the supply chain of pharmaceutical corporations were screened and checked against debarment lists. In determining which contracting businesses to work with, particularly for transportation and warehousing, corporations in the pharmaceutical industry also sometimes consulted with each other.

Another issue that often came up in discussions was that of *who* conducted the screening and vetting of potential candidates during the hiring process. Several corporations interviewed used a third-party vendor for all or part of the screening process. Some third-party vendors specialize in one aspect of the screening, such as a background check or drug test. Vendors were also more likely to be used when public records required manual collection—for example, from state

---

8   For an example from the service industry, see John E. G. Bateson, "Psychometric Sifting to Efficiently Select the Right Service Employees," *Managing Service Quality*, Vol. 24, No. 5, 2014.

9   For technical details of how this technique works, see S. S. Alduayj and P. Smith, "Sentiment Classification and Prediction of Job Interview Performance," *2019 2nd International Conference on Computer Applications & Information Security (ICCAIS)*, Riyadh, Saudi Arabia, May 1–3, 2019.

courthouses. Other vendors were noted to be widely used for certain industries, such as finance, where they had agreements to access the FBI database. This is similar to USG use of a shared service provider, such as DCSA performing the investigative role for 95 percent of executive agencies.

Posthire Monitoring and Evaluation

Once employees are hired, corporations turn to monitoring and evaluation techniques to guard against risk and address events that result in losses or damages (Figure 4.3). The term of art that the USG uses for this process is CE,[10] with Trusted Workforce 2.0 rolling out a construct called CV.[11] Several corporations in our sample described unique, customized approaches to employee monitoring and associated detection and mitigation of threats, while others interviewed followed standard business practices that are associated with talent management (e.g., following up on issues brought to HR, including placement of employees on performance improvement plans).

Corporations across all sectors included standard talent management as part of their employee monitoring process. Several firms interviewed, especially smaller corporations and start-ups, did little more than routine manager check-ins and employee performance evaluations. If anything, these corporations either were moving or have moved away from an annual review to make assessments more frequent and distributed throughout the year. Basic employee management included annual security awareness training and other trainings as a form of risk mitigation, for example, on workplace violence and harassment. The security awareness trainings were designed to mini-

---

10 A previous RAND report covers CE extensively, including its history, legislative context, theoretical underpinnings, current evidence for effectiveness, and cost (Luckey et al., 2019).

11 CV involves automated record checks with agency-specific data sources (e.g., insider threat, self-reporting, incident reports), along with related fieldwork and data checks. The idea behind CV is to build a collaboration between HR, security, and other partner missions across the organization to provide a more holistic vetting and monitoring approach for the USG.

Figure 4.3
Posthire Monitoring and Remediation of Risk

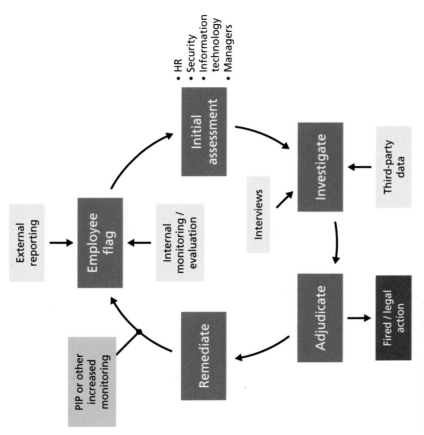

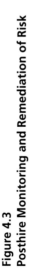

SOURCE: RAND analysis of corporate interviews.
NOTES: Blue = major steps; yellow = flag or initial investigation; orange = increased monitoring; red = termination. PIP = performance improvement plan.

mize the number of insider threats perpetrated because of negligence or ignorance, while workplace conduct training focused on workplace violence and abuse, encouraging peer reporting. Other related trainings, such as "active aggressor" trainings, were designed not because such events were considered likely, but primarily to assuage employee concerns. One finance corporation in our sample reported sending test emails aligned with the principles of the security awareness training to check whether employees were following best practices.

Five of the larger corporations in the pharmaceutical, finance, and gaming sectors employed additional monitoring strategies to proactively identify potentially risky behaviors or threat of misconduct. These were mostly aimed at identifying insider cyber threats or using electronic means to identify threats. This included monitoring emails, social media, and other publicly accessible information, as well as conducting system-wide audits for anomalous activity. One gaming corporation interviewed had dedicated personnel to monitor social media accounts daily for suspicious behaviors in employee postings, ranging from violent tendencies to publicly sharing proprietary information. Another corporation interviewed conducted continuous analysis of high-profile and high-risk personnel using screenshots from their computers and emails and tracked other corporations through open-source material to watch for potential IP theft or defection to other corporations. Financial entities mentioned tracking time spent in client accounts, and another corporation in our sample emphasized inventory monitoring across supply chain facilities and warehouses. The objective of cyber monitoring was to look for irregularities in activity or behavior, particularly relative to averages across all employees. One corporation also had an internal unit dedicated to auditing its contracting staff.

Additional employee monitoring strategies employed by our sample included monitoring the physical environment for threats. Financial sector interviewees noted the issue of having many physical branch locations that must be actively monitored for entry and exit, especially at off-hours. One larger financial entity interviewed described an internal center, along with an internal cyber threat management center, that was designated specifically for physical security risk management. Similar to formal cyber monitoring systems, this monitoring was semiautonomous, and any "unusual" activity triggered an alert for further investigation. One pharmaceutical corporation had a similar system that would lead to alerts and follow-up if production and supply chain counts exceeded certain expectable bounds. And gaming corporations used continuous video monitoring of all customer service locations with a separate, dedicated security team that was completely "firewalled" from HR or other corporate functions.

All but one of the corporations interviewed described informal *human intelligence* networks (e.g., current and former employees) that provided informal reporting on unusual behavior and other potential employee threats in the workplace. Several interviewees believed it was important for HR representatives to actively engage with employees to identify potential personal and professional stressors. One interviewee believed HR representatives could eventually act as counselors for staff when appropriate. Similarly, one interviewee noted offering contracted counseling support for employees if they were going through a tough time or if they were being let go.

The majority of corporations across sectors relied on traditional means for employee monitoring, consisting of whistleblowers, managers, or colleagues reporting suspicious behaviors or concerning life events or circumstances. For example, a manager could let HR know if an employee were going through contentious divorce, or if a minimum wage employee had purchased a brand new luxury car. One interviewee described having considered calls from external parties reporting suspicious behaviors and decided on a case-by-case basis whether the claims were worth pursuing. In addition to reporting concerns to HR, at least one interviewee noted formal channels, including a hotline, by which worrisome employee behaviors or actions could be reported.

Our interviews indicated that internal divisions among corporate functions (for example, between security and HR in the gaming industry) could prevent adoption of intelligence fusion and integrative decisionmaking. Meanwhile, corporations where security, HR, and other functions were highly integrated (or even fused under the direction of a single executive) seemed to facilitate both the use of informal intelligence gathering and newer AI and ML approaches.

When a concern was raised about an employee, most firms interviewed took action on a case-by-case basis. They reviewed the complaint and employee record to determine whether it was worth pursuing. If an investigation was opened, it was generally a collaboration between HR and security. HR would conduct interviews with the employee's manager and colleagues, while security might run new screens and checks on suspicious activity. Security might also search for new hits on public records or look for validating content on social media accounts, blogs, and other public forums or online discussion boards. Depending on the nature of the concern, there would be an internal deliberation and decision on how to proceed.

Legal and other policy considerations influenced how interviewees across sectors dealt with employee monitoring and insider threat management. As with screening and vetting, some of the more regulated firms focused on regulatory compliance. This was highlighted in our interviews with financial firms insured by FDIC, which conducts regular audits that include mitigation of insider threats. Concerns mentioned by other interviewees related to more-advanced CE practices included reporting requirements; investment in data infrastructure; data management; available technical talent to program, monitor, and conduct investigations; and algorithmic bias if using ML or other automated big-data analytic techniques.

As with screening and vetting, in many cases, it was not one single entity that was responsible for employee monitoring and insider threat management, but a collaboration between HR, security (including physical and information security), and other functions.[12] Some corporations had formalized processes, and some had central investigative units and dedicated monitoring personnel. One corporation worked with a third-party vendor to obtain investigative information, such as rerunning background checks or gathering publicly available information. Corporations in the pharmaceutical and gaming sectors mentioned networking informally with each other to occasionally share intelligence about the threat environment. And one gaming corporation mentioned regular, formal meetings to share intelligence with law enforcement entities and other state and federal agencies regarding the evolving threat environment.

Our discussions revealed a notable range in corporate organization models for managing insider threats. The range in organizational models appeared to correlate with the organization's CE processes in place, and with assigned roles and responsibilities in addressing potential threats. These models include

---

12   General Counsel was also involved, although this seemed to be only when cases reached a certain threshold.

- central employee threat monitoring center or hub, with tech-driven monitoring
- insider risk management committee convened by senior leadership across units
- constant collaboration between security and HR
- frequent collaboration between security and external human intelligence information providers
- no specified organizational structure associated with insider threats or CE.

Finally, especially for large organizations, our discussions also raised the question of the level of centralization. That is, whether threat management should be completely centralized or organized for each unit, program, or office. In the gaming industry, for example, security is usually completely separate from HR, with no personal interaction and little to no data sharing. In other corporations, HR and security functions were essentially fused.[13]

Overall, few corporations in our sample used newer AI and ML automated analysis approaches for prehire screening, vetting, or employee monitoring that have received considerable media attention. Our interviews indicated that internal divisions among corporate functions (for example, between security and HR in the gaming industry) could prevent deployment of such approaches. Meanwhile, smaller corporations where security, HR, and other functions were highly integrated (or even fused under the direction of a single executive) seemed to facilitate the use of newer AI and ML approaches.

---

13 The gaming industry has specific cash flow vulnerabilities that have traditionally mandated this firewall between security and HR. But even this seems to be breaking down over time to leverage data sharing for joint efforts in early risk detection. As much as possible, data sharing and consultation across the corporate enterprise seems to optimize both detection and decisionmaking.

Conclusion

In terms of employee roles presenting the greatest risk, corporations across industry sectors most consistently mentioned: (1) high-level executives whose behaviors could expose the corporation to reputational risk or vulnerability via blackmail; and (2) HR, information technology, or other administrative personnel with access to client and personnel data as well as (in some cases) corporate IP. Meanwhile, the most frequently mentioned motivation for nefarious employee behavior was disgruntlement and vengeance, which could lead to theft of corporate property or even threats to workplace safety.

Corporations in our sample exhibited considerable diversity in screening, vetting, and monitoring practices, much of which was industry-specific and some of which was more related to legacy versus nonlegacy status (corporate size and stage of growth). For example, smaller and newer corporations preferred less-structured, more-flexible and informal screening and vetting processes, with any malfeasance handled on a case-by-case basis. Larger organizations in established, highly regulated industries, such as finance and pharmaceuticals, tended to have more-structured processes, owing to the constant need to follow federal and state regulations.

Few corporations in our sample used newer AI and ML automated analysis approaches for prehire screening and vetting or employee monitoring that have received considerable media attention. Integration of corporate functions and overall corporate agility seem to be critical for employing such approaches. Corporations that did employ AI or ML techniques cautioned that any automated analytics needed constant monitoring and contextualized interpretation with a "human in the loop." We pursue this theme further in the next chapter.

CHAPTER FIVE

Conclusions and Insights

Private corporations and the USG share many of the same challenges in terms of vulnerability to insider threat and the need to screen, vet, and monitor individuals. However, as noted previously (see Chapter Two, the section on "Conclusions and Lessons for Comparison"), the practices of private corporations also differ significantly from the USG personnel security vetting process. Specifically, private corporations must customize their screening, vetting, and monitoring processes to conform to (sometimes quite specific, federally mandated) industry-specific requirements, but they can and do also customize components of the talent cycle to conform to corporation-specific threats and vulnerabilities.

That said, it is possible to draw some broad comparative lessons from our corporate research for the USG as it continues to reform the personnel security vetting process. These insights come from the ways in which private corporations described their current processes for screening, vetting, and monitoring, as well as how these processes have changed over time, and how corporate security and HR professionals see these processes adapting to the future threat environment. Such insights also come from discussions with our interviewees about what they think the USG should consider as it modernizes its own processes.

As mentioned in Chapter Three, these findings are subject to several methodological challenges that limit their generalizability, including potential response bias among corporations willing to be interviewed for this research. Still, the common themes we identified may be useful illustrations of how corporations with relevant characteristics assess and monitor employees. Here, we offer a number of insights derived from our research to inform how the USG may be able to take advantage of this corporate perspective.

Insights

1. *Proper triage of potential insider threats is challenging but critical.* Our respondents described the increasing trend toward carefully sorting potential threats into cases that can be addressed with HR or other approaches versus cases that require immediate punitive action. Potentially derogatory information on those who work for or on behalf of the federal government presents a wide range of response options. With both the threat environment and the information environment rapidly expanding, proper sorting of these cases is challenging but necessary to maintain a balance between preserving operational capacity and eliminating critical threats.

In both our background research[1] and interviews, we noted an emphasis on using a broad range of corporate resources to respond to potentially derogatory information with early intervention when possible. Respondents recognized the need to terminate or take legal action against severe, active threats—for example, those who are already leaking data to competitors or foreign adversaries, or those who are found to be actively planning violent action. However, we also heard how continuous monitoring of employees—whether driven by social media data or human intelligence—presents opportunities for early intervention that may offset later risk. For example, potential "red flags," such as financial debt, could present opportunities for corporations to provide assistance to employees so that these situations did not worsen

---

1   For example, see minutes 36–39 in Intelligence and National Security Alliance, "2019 Summit: Continuous Evaluation: Balancing Security & Privacy Panel," video, YouTube, September 24, 2019.

over time.[2] The success of this early identification and triage depends critically on intelligence fusion, which is our next recommendation.

2. *Share intelligence inside and outside the organization.* HR and security professionals described a variety of creative ways to fuse and share intelligence to rapidly identify and address emerging threats.

We learned from our interview respondents how properly identifying insider threats at any stage of the talent lifecycle requires a multifaceted, collaborative approach. Interviews emphasized that optimizing this process requires that (at the minimum) HR and security functions actively share data and engage in joint decisionmaking. One respondent described a truly fused HR and security function in which employees are constantly engaged in "soft touch" human interactions in concert with constant internal monitoring of information systems. This could be extended to include legal, compliance, and other corporate functions. Other respondents described regular threat assessment meetings with regulatory and law enforcement bodies, as well as other corporations in the same sector.

Of course, productive intelligence fusion and shared decision-making take work, whether in the form of extra labor or even structural institutional changes. And such fusion is subject to legal and regulatory constraints, especially when conducted by the USG. Emerging technologies may help lower the labor costs of intelligence fusion.[3] However, these are still in their infancy and should be employed with caution and human monitoring, which is our next recommendation.

---

2 The USG also seems to be headed in this direction with Trusted Workforce 2.0, which employs a "Whole of Person" concept and has recently released guidance on ensuring that cleared employees suffering financially from the COVID-19 pandemic are not unduly punished for reasons outside of their own control.

3 For an overview, see Erik Blasch, Ivan Kadar, Lynne Grewe, Garrett Stevenson, Uttam Majumder, and Chee-Yee Chong, "Deep Learning in AI and Information Fusion Panel Discussion," *Proceedings* Vol. 11018, Signal Processing, Sensor/Information Fusion, and Target Recognition XXVIII, SPIE Defense + Commercial Sensing, Baltimore, Md., 2019. For an example, see Kehua Guo, Tao Xu, Xiaoyan Kui, Ruifang Zhang, and Tao Chi, "iFusion: Towards Efficient Intelligence Fusion for Deep Learning from Real-Time and Heterogeneous Data," *Information Fusion*, Vol. 51, November 1, 2019.

3. *A human in the loop is essential.* For the foreseeable future, automated algorithms to detect risky or nefarious behavior by applicants or those who work for or on behalf of the federal government need significant, consistent oversight by HR or security professionals.

The use of AI and ML approaches to categorize (much less predict) human behavior through the analysis of text and other data is still in its early stages. Much as algorithms struggle to properly understand nuance in social media posts,[4] using ML to sort human behavior into categories (such as flagging nefarious behavior) is rife with risks for error and bias.[5] Automated algorithms, even those that are trained with human-coded data, run the risk of building upon preexisting biases in human judgment,[6] as well as misclassification through missing crucial subtleties in context.[7] According to interviewees who have used these tools, thresholds for "red flags" must be constantly recalibrated to keep up with changes in corporate operations, the information environment, and the nature of threats themselves. Because of the potential for such error (e.g., false positives or negatives that can result in bias), humans are needed to interpret and adjudicate algorithmic results.

Furthermore, automated systems can be "gamed" by individuals who either gain access to the algorithm, successfully guess the way in which automated algorithms function, or learn how to manipulate the

---

4   Natasha Duarte, Emma Llansó, and Anna Loup, "Mixed Messages? The Limits of Automated Social Media Content Analysis," paper presented at 2018 Conference on Fairness, Accountability, and Transparency, New York, February 23–24, 2018.

5   Katharina A. Zweig, Georg Wenzelburger, and Tobias D. Krafft, "On Chances and Risks of Security Related Algorithmic Decision Making Systems," *European Journal for Security Research*, Vol. 3, No. 2, October 1, 2018.

6   Bruno Lepri, Nuria Oliver, Emmanuel Letouzé, Alex Pentland, and Patrick Vinck, "Fair, Transparent, and Accountable Algorithmic Decision-Making Processes," *Philosophy and Technology*, Vol. 31, No. 4, December 2018.

7   For further discussion of the limitations of automated approaches to threat detection in the CE context, see pp. 31–33 in Luckey et al., 2019.

system through trial and error.[8] The possibility for automated systems for computer vision, speech recognition, and other modalities to be hacked in this way has been well documented,[9] and similar issues with gaming automated screening and hiring processes have been noted in the talent acquisition industry.[10]

The corporations we interviewed that currently used ML to automate red flags for employee misbehavior, sorting applicants, or any other purposes emphasized to us that manual oversight, calibration, and checking of these processes was a constant necessity. Part of this was because of the perpetually evolving nature of corporate operations, information systems, and the threat environment itself. At most, such systems are currently practical only for referring cases to human personnel for further checking and triage.

4. Taking a "whole of community" approach to identifying and mitigating threats helps share labor burden and improves effectiveness. Corporations emphasized the importance of a customized, flexible, "hands-on" approach to threat detection and mitigation. To take advantage of existing corporate practices and data streams, the USG could develop requirements for critical information and task corporate intelligence, HR, and security functions to provide that information with the appropriate caveats and context.

---

8   The simplest example of this is resume "keyword stacking." For example, see Alison Doyle, "Tips for Using Resume Keywords," *The Balance: Careers*, February 19, 2020. Similarly, if an employee can access automated thresholds for red flags in supply chain anomalies, then theft can be calibrated to occur just under this threshold.

9   For example, see M. Mihajlović and N. Popović, "Fooling a Neural Network with Common Adversarial Noise," *2018 19th IEEE Mediterranean Electrotechnical Conference (MELECON)*, Marrakech, Morocco, May 2–7, 2018. It should be noted that some of these hacks can also fool time-limited human decisionmakers. For example, see Gamaleldin Elsayed, Shreya Shankar, Brian Cheung, Nicolas Papernot, Alexey Kurakin, Ian Goodfellow, and Jascha Sohl-Dickstein, "Adversarial Examples That Fool Both Computer Vision and Time-Limited Humans," paper presented at the 32nd Conference on Neural Information Processing Systems, Montreal, Canada, December 2–8, 2018.

10   For example, see Donna Moores, "The Pros and Cons of Recruitment Automation," *we the talent blog*, TALENTSOFT, July 3, 2017.

The USG will continue to rely on a wide variety of government and nongovernment entities that employ clearance-holders and others in the interest of national security and other positions of public trust. The USG already works with nongovernment employers to help monitor cleared individuals, but the role played by nongovernment employers could be considerably expanded in years to come. For instance, nongovernment employers may analyze information sources, such as social media posts, to gain a more nuanced view of these individuals. Because the government may lack the capacity to perform similar analyses, this additional context would not only help share the labor burden, but would also provide more contextualized and likely more accurate information on which—among those who work for or on behalf of the federal government—are critical threats (as opposed to individuals who exhibit temporary red flags for understandable or addressable reasons). While centralized data sources and collection by the USG will continue to play a role, the USG may also wish to consider asking corporations and other entities to provide ground-level perspectives on critical information categories—for example, allegiance to the United States, lack of inappropriate substance use, and proper control over financial debt.

Through mandating certain practices and asking for data streams from employers, the USG could maintain a centralized set of standards while allowing local application of best practices for screening and vetting to identify potential threats. There are signs that the transformation of the USG screening, vetting, and monitoring process is developing a more flexible framework for understanding risk with its shift toward CE and CV.[11] As we learn more about what works in certain industries, the USG may wish to consider the extent to which it should mandate certain hiring, screening, vetting, and monitoring processes in its various military, intelligence, other federal, and private corporate partners. These mandates could require that successful approaches be deployed in certain contexts while allowing for flexibility at the local level.

11 Ogrysko, 2019b.

Future Directions

A quick scan of private industry and consulting solutions for attracting, hiring, screening, vetting, and monitoring employees reveals a panoply of automated tools promising to increase the efficiency and accuracy of insider threat detection. Our research suggests that private corporations have not yet employed such approaches in a widespread fashion. Furthermore, any corporations that currently use or have experimented with such technology caution that they need constant human labor to calibrate these automated systems and place their findings in context to determine appropriate next steps.

There is little doubt that the potential threats posed by employees are growing in their diversity and possible severity,[12] prompted in part by the growing sophistication of foreign adversaries seeking to place or recruit such threats inside the United States. In the face of these challenges, traditional approaches to screening, vetting, and monitoring using mostly human labor may no longer be sufficient. However, the wide variety of automated AI- and ML-based "solutions" currently offered in industry (or suggested by academic studies) have not yet been systematically tested or assessed.

For the USG to make effective decisions about how to incorporate emerging technology into its new screening, vetting, and monitoring process, it will be important to place the various promises offered by the emerging AI/ML HR industry and new academic studies in applied, real-world context. This would require examining how these emerging approaches operate (including how they are similar and different from one another), as well as assessing their real-world effectiveness in successfully identifying threats.

Failure to adopt emerging approaches to screening, vetting, and monitoring could leave the USG exposed in the evolving threat environment. However, failing to undertake a systematic review and assessment of these approaches could lead to wasted investment, acquisition of ineffective systems that miss important threats or misidentify harmless behaviors as threats, or potentially even deepen existing bias and discrimination in current HR systems.

---

12 *Insider Threat Report: Out of Sight Should Never Be out of Mind*, 2019.

Interview Codes

- Highest-Risk Personnel
  - Admin/operations workers
  - All workers equally
  - Contractors
  - Front-line workers
  - Senior-level management
- Minimizing Risk—Post-Event
  - Providing support service
  - Stakeholder engagement
  - Working with employee
- Mitigating Risk—Monitoring
  - Legal and other considerations
  - Proactive monitoring
  - Reactive monitoring
  - Threat management organization
- Mitigating Risk—Prehire
  - Qualifying criteria/attributes
- Mitigating Risk—Screening/Vetting
  - Background checks
  - Other screening activities
  - Personality screening
  - Training of HR/security screeners
- Risk Management—Staff and Training
- Types of Risk
  - Employee risk

Fraud, dishonesty and trustworthiness
- External risk
- Threat or event
  - Cyber (intentional and unintentional)
    Money laundering
    Regulatory compliance
    Reputation
    Theft
  - Identity/PII theft
  - IP theft
  - Monetary theft
- Workplace Violence/Safety

References

2019 Talent Trends Report, Atlanta, Ga.: Randstad Sourceright, 2019. As of June 2, 2020:
https://content.randstadsourceright.com/hubfs/Global%20campaign/TTR/2019/report/Randstad-Sourceright-2019-Talent-Trends-Report-190118.pdf

Alduayj, S. S., and P. Smith, "Sentiment Classification and Prediction of Job Interview Performance," *2019 2nd International Conference on Computer Applications & Information Security (ICCAIS)*, Riyadh, Saudi Arabia, May 1–3, 2019, pp. 1–6.

BasuMallick, Chiradeep, "Gamification in Recruitment: All You Need to Know," *HR Technologist*, November 30, 2018. As of June 1, 2020:
https://www.hrtechnologist.com/articles/recruitment-onboarding/gamification-in-recruitment-all-you-need-to-know/

Bateson, John E. G., Jochen Wirtz, Eugene Burke, and Carly Vaughan, "Psychometric Sifting to Efficiently Select the Right Service Employees," *Managing Service Quality*, Vol. 24, No. 5, 2014, pp. 418–433. As of February 5, 2020:
https://doi.org/10.1108/MSQ-04-2014-0091

Bengochea, Sarah, "Putting Brand and Challenge at the Heart of Talent Acquisition," *Blog & News*, Avature, 2020. As of June 1, 2020:
https://www.avature.net/putting-brand-challenge-heart-talent-acquisition/

Bersin, Josh, "Why People Management Is Replacing Talent Management," LinkedIn, December 29, 2014. As of June 1, 2020:
https://www.linkedin.com/pulse/corporate-talent-management-dead-josh-bersin/

Blasch, Erik, Ivan Kadar, Lynne Grewe, Garrett Stevenson, Uttam Majumder, and Chee-Yee Chong, "Deep Learning in AI and Information Fusion Panel Discussion," *Proceedings* Vol. 11018, Signal Processing, Sensor/Information Fusion, and Target Recognition XXVIII, SPIE Defense + Commercial Sensing, Baltimore, Md., 2019.

Boyd, Aaron, "Security Clearance Backlog Hits Long-Awaited 'Steady State,'" *Nextgov*, January 22, 2020. As of June 1, 2020:
https://www.nextgov.com/cybersecurity/2020/01/
security-clearance-backlog-hits-long-awaited-steady-state/162593/

Cappelli, Peter, "Your Approach to Hiring Is All Wrong," *Harvard Business Review*, May–June 2019. As of June 1, 2020:
https://hbr.org/2019/05/
recruiting?ab=hero-main-text#your-approach-to-hiring-is-all-wrong

Castillo, Mariano, "Other Leakers: What Happened to Them?" CNN, January 2, 2014. As of June 1, 2020:
https://www.cnn.com/2014/01/02/us/snowden-famous-leakers/index.html

Chamberlain, Andrew, "Job Market Trends: Five Hiring Disruptions to Watch in 2019," webpage, Glassdoor, December 2018. As of June 1, 2020:
https://b2b-assets.glassdoor.com/job-market-trends-five-hiring-disruptions-to-watch-in-2019.pdf

Dawson, John, "6 Best Recruiting Tools of 2019," blog post, *AI for Recruiting: News, Tips, and Trends*, Ideal, January 10, 2019. As of June 1, 2020:
https://ideal.com/recruiting-tools/

DCSA—*See* Defense Counterintelligence and Security Agency.

Defense Counterintelligence and Security Agency Office of Public Affairs, "Background Investigation Mission Moving to DoD," press release, Office of Personnel Management, July 2019. As of December 27, 2019:
https://nbib.opm.gov/news/nbib-news/2019/07/
background-investigation-mission-moving-to-dod/

Doyle, Alison, "Tips for Using Resume Keywords," *The Balance: Careers*, February 19, 2020. As of June 1, 2020:
https://www.thebalancecareers.com/
resume-keywords-and-tips-for-using-them-2063331

Duarte, Natasha, Emma Llansó, and Anna Loup, "Mixed Messages? The Limits of Automated Social Media Content Analysis," paper presented at 2018 Conference on Fairness, Accountability, and Transparency, New York, February 23–24, 2018. As of June 1, 2020:
https://cdt.nclud.com/wp-content/uploads/2017/12/
FAT-conference-draft-2018.pdf

Elias, Jennifer, "Report: Google Management Scrambles to Contain Employee 'Uproar' over China Project," *Silicon Valley Business Journal*, August 3, 2018. As of June 1, 2020:
https://www.bizjournals.com/sanjose/news/2018/08/03/google-employees-reaction-project-dragonfly-china.html

Elsayed, Gamaleldin, Shreya Shankar, Brian Cheung, Nicolas Papernot, Alexey Kurakin, Ian Goodfellow, and Jascha Sohl-Dickstein, "Adversarial Examples That Fool Both Computer Vision and Time-Limited Humans," paper presented at the 32nd Conference on Neural Information Processing Systems, Montreal, Canada, December 2–8, 2018. As of June 1, 2020:
http://papers.nips.cc/paper/7647-adversarial-examples-that-fool-both-computer-vision-and-time-limited-humans.pdf

G2, "Best Applicant Tracking Systems," webpage, 2020. As of February 5, 2020:
https://www.g2.com/categories/applicant-tracking-systems-ats

GAO—*See* U.S. Government Accountability Office.

Grafton, Jane, "Famous Insider Threat Cases," *GURUCUL* blog, September 5, 2019. As of June 1, 2020:
https://gurucul.com/blog/famous-insider-threat-cases

Grijalva, Anthony, "7 HR Technologies for Managing the Employee Lifecycle," *Employee Benefit News*, 2020. As of June 1, 2020:
https://www.benefitnews.com/list/hr-technology-for-managing-the-employee-lifecycle

Guo, Kehua, Tao Xu, Xiaoyan Kui, Ruifang Zhang, and Tao Chi, "iFusion: Towards Efficient Intelligence Fusion for Deep Learning from Real-Time and Heterogeneous Data," *Information Fusion*, Vol. 51, November 1, 2019, pp. 215–223. As of June 1, 2020:
http://www.sciencedirect.com/science/article/pii/S1566253518304834

Harwell, Drew, "A Face-Scanning Algorithm Increasingly Decides Whether You Deserve the Job," *Washington Post*, November 6, 2019. As of June 1, 2020:
https://www.washingtonpost.com/technology/2019/10/22/ai-hiring-face-scanning-algorithm-increasingly-decides-whether-you-deserve-job/

Heckman, Jory, "ODNI Previews Updated Counterintelligence Strategy, Trusted Workforce 2.0 Rollout," *Federal News Network*, February 5, 2020. As of June 1, 2020:
https://federalnewsnetwork.com/cybersecurity/2020/02/odni-previews-updated-counterintelligence-strategy-trusted-workforce-2-0-rollout/

Insider Threat Report: Out of Sight Should Never Be Out of Mind, New York: Verizon, 2019. As of June 2, 2020:
https://enterprise.verizon.com/resources/reports/insider-threat-report.pdf

Intelligence and National Security Alliance, "2019 Summit: Continuous Evaluation: Balancing Security & Privacy Panel," video, YouTube, September 24, 2019. As of June 1, 2020:
https://www.youtube.com/watch?v=i3-Os_M59So

Kyzer, Lindy, "How Long Does It Take to Process a Security Clearance? (Q4 2019)," *ClearanceJobs*, November 20, 2019a. As of June 1, 2020:
https://news.clearancejobs.com/2019/11/20/how-long-does-it-take-to-process-a-security-clearance-q4-2019/

———, "Security Clearance Reform in the NDAA," *ClearanceJobs*, December 16, 2019b. As of June 1, 2020:
https://news.clearancejobs.com/2019/12/16/security-clearance-reform-ndaa/

Lepri, Bruno, Nuria Oliver, Emmanuel Letouzé, Alex Pentland, and Patrick Vinck, "Fair, Transparent, and Accountable Algorithmic Decision-Making Processes," *Philosophy and Technology*, Vol. 31, No. 4, December 2018, pp. 611–627. As of June 1, 2020:
https://doi.org/10.1007/s13347-017-0279-x

LexisNexis, "Perform Sanction, PEP and Watchlist Verification with Lexis Diligence," webpage, 2020. As of February 25, 2020:
https://www.lexisnexis.com/en-us/products/lexis-diligence/sanction-peps-and-watch-list-verification.page

Luckey, David, David Stebbins, Rebeca Orrie, Erin Rebhan, Sunny D. Bhatt, and Sina Beaghley, *Assessing Continuous Evaluation Approaches for Insider Threats: How Can the Security Posture of the U.S. Departments and Agencies Be Improved?* Santa Monica, Calif.: RAND Corporation, RR-2684-OSD, 2019. As of February 4, 2020:
https://www.rand.org/pubs/research_reports/RR2684.html

Marks, Joseph, "Antiquated Security Clearance Process Earns a Spot on the GAO's High-Risk List," *Nextgov*, January 25, 2018. As of June 2, 2020:
https://www.nextgov.com/cybersecurity/2018/01/hackable-vulnerabilities-long-waits-return-clearance-backlog-gao-high-risk-list/145488/

McGregor, Jena, "Your Next Job Interview May Start with a Text," *Washington Post*, November 20, 2018. As of June 2, 2020:
https://www.washingtonpost.com/business/2018/11/20/your-next-job-interview-may-start-with-text/

McMurtie, Tom, "Insider Threats: Taking a Holistic Approach to Protecting Agency Data," *Federal News Network*, December 27, 2017. As of June 2, 2020:
https://federalnewsnetwork.com/cybersecurity/2017/12/insider-threats-taking-a-holistic-approach-to-protecting-agency-data/

Mihajlović, M., and N. Popović, "Fooling a Neural Network with Common Adversarial Noise," *2018 19th IEEE Mediterranean Electrotechnical Conference (MELECON)*, Marrakech, Morocco, May 2–7, 2018, pp. 293–296.

Moores, Donna, "The Pros and Cons of Recruitment Automation," *we the talent* blog, TALENTSOFT, July 3, 2017. As of June 2, 2020:
https://www.wethetalent.co/experience-at-work/pros-and-cons-of-recruitment-automation

Office of Personnel Management, "Cybersecurity Resource Center: Cybersecurity Incidents," webpage, 2015. As of December 27, 2019:
https://www.opm.gov/cybersecurity/cybersecurity-incidents/

Ogrysko, Nicole, "'Time to Change the Rules' for the Security Clearance Process, Its Leaders Say," *Federal News Network*, August 7, 2018. As of June 2, 2020:
https://federalnewsnetwork.com/workforce/2018/08/
time-to-change-the-rules-for-the-security-clearance-process-its-leaders-say/

———, "Trump Makes Security Clearance Transfer Official with Executive Order," *Federal News Network*, April 24, 2019a. As of June 2, 2020:
https://federalnewsnetwork.com/workforce/2019/04/
trump-makes-security-clearance-transfer-official-with-executive-order/

———, "The Future of Continuous Evaluation Is Just About Here, and It Has a Different Name," *Federal News Network*, September 6, 2019b. As of June 2, 2020:
https://federalnewsnetwork.com/workforce/2019/09/
the-future-of-continuous-evaluation-is-just-about-here-and-it-has-a-different-name/

———, "Congress Catches Up on Security Clearance Modernization Efforts in NDAA," *Federal News Network*, December 12, 2019c. As of June 2, 2020:
https://federalnewsnetwork.com/defense-news/2019/12/
congress-catches-up-on-security-clearance-modernization-efforts-in-ndaa/

Okyere, Mike Kofi, "Recruitment Analytics: How Data Helps Achieve Better Results," webpage, Recruiter, July 30, 2018. As of June 2, 2020:
https://www.recruiter.com/i/
recruitment-analytics-how-data-helps-achieve-better-results/

Ong, Michelle, and Mike Rote, "FINRA Fines Citigroup Global Markets Inc. $1.25 Million for Failing to Appropriately Fingerprint or Screen Employees over Seven-Year Period," press release, FINRA, July 29, 2019. As of June 2, 2020:
https://www.finra.org/media-center/newsreleases/2019/
finra-fines-citigroup-global-markets-inc-125-million-employee-screening

OPM—*See* Office of Personnel Management.

PA Consulting Group, *Holistic Management of Employee Risk (HoMER)*, London: Centre for the Protection of National Infrastructure, 2012. As of June 3, 2020:
https://www.cpni.gov.uk/system/files/documents/62/53/Holistic-Management-of-
Employee-Risk-HoMER-Guidance.pdf

Ponemon Institute, *2018 Cost of Insider Threats: Global Study*, Boston, Mass.: ObserveIT, April 2018.

Public Law 111-203, Dodd-Frank Wall Street Reform and Consumer Protection Act, July 21, 2010.

"Push to Change Security Clearance Policies Underway," *FEDweek*, August 21, 2019. As of June 1, 2020:
https://www.fedweek.com/fedweek/changes-to-security-clearance-policies-considered/

Society for Human Resource Management, "Conducting Background Investigations and Reference Checks," webpage, 2020. As of May 14, 2020:
https://www.shrm.org/resourcesandtools/tools-and-samples/toolkits/pages/conductingbackgroundinvestigations.aspx

Stephan, Michael, David Brown, and Robin Erickson, "Talent Acquisition: Enter the Cognitive Recruiter," *Deloitte Insights*, 2017. As of June 2, 2020:
https://www2.deloitte.com/us/en/insights/focus/human-capital-trends/2017/predictive-hiring-talent-acquisition.html

Trump, Donald J., Executive Order on Transferring Responsibility for Background Investigations to the Department of Defense, April 24, 2019. As of June 2, 2020:
https://www.whitehouse.gov/presidential-actions/executive-order-transferring-responsibility-background-investigations-department-defense/

U.S. Department of Defense, *Department of Defense Suitability and Fitness Guide: Procedures and Guidance for Civilian Employment Suitability and Fitness Determinations Within the Department of Defense*, Washington, D.C., updated July 28, 2016. As of June 1, 2020:
https://www.dhra.mil/Portals/52/Documents/perserec/DoD_Suitability_Guide_Version_1.0.pdf

U.S. Government Accountability Office, "Information Security: Agencies Need to Improve Controls over Selected High-Impact Systems," GAO-16-501, Washington, D.C., June 21, 2016. As of June 2, 2020:
https://www.gao.gov/products/GAO-16-501

———, "Information Security: OPM Has Improved Controls, but Further Efforts Are Needed," GAO-17-614, Washington, D.C., August 3, 2017a. As of June 2, 2020:
https://www.gao.gov/products/GAO-17-614

———, "Personnel Security Clearances: Plans Needed to Fully Implement and Oversee Continuous Evaluation of Clearance Holders," GAO-18-117, Washington, D.C., November 21, 2017b. As of June 2, 2020:
https://www.gao.gov/products/GAO-18-117

———, "Personnel Security Clearances: Additional Actions Needed to Ensure Quality, Address Timeliness, and Reduce Investigation Backlog," GAO-18-29, Washington, D.C., December 12, 2017c. As of June 2, 2020:
https://www.gao.gov/products/GAO-18-29

———, "Personnel Security Clearances: Additional Actions Needed to Implement Key Reforms and Improve Timely Processing of Investigations," GAO-18-431T, Washington, D.C., March 7, 2018. As of June 2, 2020:
https://www.gao.gov/products/GAO-18-431T

Vasilogambros, Matt, and *National Journal*, "The Navy Yard Shooting Could Have Been Prevented, Review Finds," *The Atlantic*, March 18, 2014. As of June 2, 2020:
https://www.theatlantic.com/politics/archive/2014/03/
the-navy-yard-shooting-could-have-been-prevented-review-finds/437502/

Verizon, "VERIS: The Vocabulary for Event Recording and Incident Sharing," webpage, 2019. As of February 5, 2020:
http://veriscommunity.net/index.html

Volini, Erica, Jeff Schwartz, and Indranil Roy, "Accessing Talent: It's More Than Acquisition," *Deloitte Insights*, 2018.

Wolfe, Jan, Joseph Ax, David Ingram, Kevin Drawbaugh, and Jonathan Oatis, "Factbox: Long History of U.S. Leakers to Media Facing Charges," Reuters, August 4, 2017. As of June 2, 2020:
https://www.reuters.com/article/us-usa-trump-sessions-leaks-factbox/
factbox-long-history-of-u-s-leakers-to-media-facing-charges-idUSKBN1AK294

Zweig, Katharina A., Georg Wenzelburger, and Tobias D. Krafft, "On Chances and Risks of Security Related Algorithmic Decision Making Systems," *European Journal for Security Research*, Vol. 3, No. 2, October 1, 2018, pp. 181–203. As of June 2, 2020:
https://doi.org/10.1007/s41125-018-0031-2